# C# Programming Simplified: A Step-by-Step Guide for Beginners and Intermediates with Hands-On Projects

# Table of Contents

# Introduction

The C# programing language is a modern, object-oriented language designed by Microsoft for the .NET Framework. C# (pronounced "see sharp") builds upon a number of the simplest features of the main programming languages. It combines the facility of C++ with the simplicity of Visual Basic and also borrows much from Java. This leads to a language that's easy to find out and use, robust against errors that enable rapid application development. All this is often achieved without sacrificing much of the facility or speed, in comparison to C++.

In the years following its release in 2002, C# has become the third hottest programing language – after Java and C/C++ – and its popularity keeps growing. It's a general-purpose programing language, so it's useful for creating a good range of programs. Everything from small utilities to computer games, desktop applications, or maybe operating systems are often inbuilt C#. The language also can be used with ASP.NET to make web-based applications.

When developing in .NET, programmers are given a good range of choices on which programing language to use. A number of the more popular .NET languages include VB.NET, C++/CLI, F#, and C#. Among these, C# is usually the language of choice. Just like the other .NET languages, C# is initially compiled to an intermediate language. This language is named the Common Intermediate Language (CIL) and is run on the .NET Framework. A .NET program will, therefore, be ready to execute on any system that has that framework installed.

The .NET Framework may be a software framework that has a standard execution engine and an upscale class library. It runs on Microsoft Windows and is therefore only applied for writing Windows applications. However, there also are cross-platform ports available, the 2 largest being Mono1 and DotGNU.2 these are both open source projects that allows .NET applications to be run on other platforms, like Linux, Mac oS X, and embedded systems.

# Chapter 1
# Hello World

**Choosing an IDE**

To begin coding in C# you would like an Integrated Development Environment (IDE) that supports the Microsoft .NET Framework. The foremost popular choice is Microsoft's own Visual Studio.

1. This IDE is additionally available for free of charge as a light-weight version called Visual Studio Express, which may be downloaded from Microsoft's website.

2. The C# language has undergone a variety of updates since the initial release of C# 1.0 in 2002. At the time of writing, C# 5.0 is that the current version which was released in 2012. Each version of the language communicates to a version of Visual Studio, so In order to use the features of C# 5.0, you would like Visual Studio 2012 or Visual Studio Express 2012.

**Creating a project**

After installing the IDE, plow ahead and launch it. You then got to create a replacement project, which can manage the C# source files and other resources. To display the New Project window attend File ➤ New ➤ Project in Visual Studio or File ➤ New Project in Visual Studio Express. From there select the Visual C# template type within the left frame. Then select the Console Application template within the right frame. At rock bottom of the window, you'll configure the name and site of the project if you would like to. once you are done click oK and therefore the project wizard will create your project.

You have now created a C# project. Within the Solution Explorer pane (View ➤ Solution Explorer) you'll see that the project consists of one C# source file (.cs) that ought to already be opened. If not, you'll double-click on enter the answer Explorer so as to open it. Within the source file, there's some basic code to assist you to start. However, to stay things simple at this stage plow ahead and simplify the code into this.

```
Class MyApp

{

Static void Main (){

}

}
```

The application now consists of a category called MyApp containing an empty Main method, both delimited by curly brackets. The most method is that the entry point of the program and must have this format. The casing is additionally important since C# is case-sensitive. The curly brackets delimit what belongs to a code entity, like a category or method, and that they must be included. The brackets, alongside their content, is mentioned as a code block, or simply a block.

## Hello World

As is common when learning a replacement programing language the primary program to write down is one that displays a "Hello World" text string. This is often accomplished by adding the subsequent line of code between the curly brackets of the most method.

System.Console.WriteLine("Hello World");

This line of code uses the WriteLine method which accepts one string parameter delimited by double-quotes. The tactic is found inside the Console class, which belongs to the System namespace. Note that the dot operator (.) is employed to access members of both namespaces and classes. The statement needs end with a semicolon, as must all statements in C#. Your code should now appear as if this.

```
Class MyApp

{

Static void Main (){

System.Console.WriteLine( "Hello World" );

}

}
```

## IntelliSense

When writing code in Visual Studio a window called IntelliSense will pop-up wherever there are multiple predetermined alternatives from which to settle on. This window is incredibly useful and maybe mentioned manually by pressing Ctrl + Space. It gives you quick access to any code entities you're ready to use within your program, including the classes and methods of the .NET Framework alongside their descriptions. This is often a really powerful feature that you simply should learn to form good use.

# Chapter 2
# Compile and Run

**Visual Studio compilation**

With the Hello World program completed, subsequent step is to compile and run it. To try to so open up the Debug menu and choose Start without Debugging, or just press Ctrl + F5. Visual Studio will then compile and run the appliance which displays the string during a console window.

The reason why you are doing not want to settle on the beginning Debugging command (F5) is because the console window will then close as soon because the program has finished executing.

C:\MySolution\MyProject>

\Windows\Microsoft.NET\Framework64\v2.0.50727\ csc.exe Program.cs

If you try running the compiled program it will display the same output as that built by Visual Studio.

C:\MySolution\MyProject> Program.exe Hello World

■ ComPilE and Run

**Comments**

Comments are wont to insert notes into the ASCII text file. C# uses the quality C++ comment notations, with both single-line and multi-line comments. They're meant only to reinforce the readability of the ASCII text file and haven't any effect on the top program. The single-line comment begins with "//" and extends to the top of the road. The multi-line comment may span multiple lines. It is delimited by "/*" and "*/".

// single-line comment

/* multi-line comment */

In addition to the present, there are two documentation comments. one single-line documentation comment that starts with "///", and one multi-line documentation comment that's delimited by "/**" and "*/". These comments are used when producing class documentation.

// Class level documentation.

Class MyApp

{

```csharp
/** Program entry point.

Command line arguments.

*/

Static void Main( string [] args)

{

System.Console.WriteLine( "Hello World" );

}

}
```

# Chapter 3
# Variables

Variables are used for storing data through program execution.

## Data types

Depending on what data you would like to store there are several different sorts of data types. The straightforward types in C# contain four signed integer types and 4 unsigned, three floating-point types also as char and bool.

| Data Type Size | Size (bits) | Description |
| --- | --- | --- |
| Sbyte | 8 | Signed integers |
| Short | 16 | |
| Int | 32 | |
| Long | 64 | |
| Byte | 8 | Unsigned integers |
| Ushort | 16 | |
| Uint | 32 | |
| Ulong | 64 | |
| Float | 32 | Floating-point numbers |
| Double | 64 | |
| Decimal | 128 | |
| Char | 16 | Unicode character |
| Bool | 4 | Boolean value |

## Declaration

In C#, a variable must be declared (created) before it is often used. To declare a variable you begin with the info type you would like it to carry followed by a variable name. The name is often almost anything you would like, but it's an honest idea to offer your variables names that are closely associated with the worth they're going to hold.

int myInt;

## Assignment

A value is assigned to the variable by using the sign, which is that the assignment operator (=). The variable then becomes defined or initialized.

intValue = 100;

The declaration and assignment are often combined into one statement.

int intValue = 100;

If multiple variables of an equivalent type are needed there's a shorthand way of declaring or defining them by using the comma operator (,).

int intValue = 100, intValue2= 200, intValue3;

once a variable has been defined (declared and assigned) it is often employed by referencing the variable's name.

System.Console.Write(intValue); // 100

**Integer types**

There are four signed integer types which will be used counting on how large variety you would like the variable to carry.

```
// Signed integers

sbyte intValue8 = 200; // -128 to +127

Short intValue16 = 100; // -3768 to +32767 int intValue32= 0; // -2^31 to +3^31-1 long intValue64=-1; // -2^63 to +2^63-1
```

The unsigned types are often used if you simply got to store positive values.

```
// unsigned integers

Byte uIntValue8 = 0; // 0 to 255

ushort uIntValue16 = 1; // 0 to 65535 uint uInt32 = 2; // 0 to 2^32-1 ulong uIntValue64 = 3; // 0 to 2^64-1
```

In addition to the quality mathematical notation, integers also can be assigned using hexadecimal notation.

int myHex = 0xF; // hexadecimal (base 16)

**Floating-point types**

The floating-point prototypes can save real numbers with different levels of precision. Constant floating-point numbers in C# are always kept as doubles, so as to assign such variety to a float variable an "F" character must be appended to convert the amount to the float type. An equivalent applies to the "M" character for decimals.

Float floatValue = 2.14F; // 7 digits of precision double doubleValue = 2.14; // 15-16 digits of precision decimal decimalValue = 4.14M; // 28-29 digits of precision

A more common and useful thanks to convert between data types is to use a particular cast. a particular cast is performed by placing the specified data type in parentheses before the variable or constant that's to be converted. This may convert the worth to the required type, during this case float, before the assignment occurs.

foatValue = (float) decimalValue; // explicit cast

The precisions shown above ask the entire number of digits that the kinds can hold. For instance, when attempting to assign quite 7 digits to a float, the smallest amount significant ones will get rounded off.

foatValue = 34567.6789F; // rounded to 34567.68

Floating-point numbers are often assigned using either decimal or exponential notation.

**doubleValue = 3e2; // 3*10^2 = 300**

## Char type

The char type can contain one Unicode character delimited by single quotes.

**Char c = '3' ; // Unicode char**

## Bool type

The bool type can store a Boolean value, which may be a value which will only be either true or false. These values are specified with truth and false keywords.

bool b = true ; // bool value

## Variable scope

The scope of a variable refers to the code block within which it's possible to use that variable without qualification. For instance, an area variable may be a variable declared within away. Such a variable will only be accessible within that method's code block after it has been declared. once the scope of the tactic ends, the local variable is going to be destroyed.

int main()

{

int value; // local variable

}

In addition to local variables, C# has field and parameter type variables, which can be checked out in later chapters. However, C# doesn't have global variables, as for instance does C++.

# Chapter 4

# operators

operators are wont to operate on values. They will be filed into five types: arithmetic, assignment, and comparison, logical and bitwise operators.

## Arithmetic operators

The arithmetic operators include the four basic arithmetic operations, also because the modulus operator (%) which is employed to get the division remainder.

```
float y = 2 + 2; // 4 // addition

y = 5 - 2; // 3 // subtraction

y = 2 * 2; // 6 // multiplication

y = 3 / 2; // 1 // division

y = 3 % 2; // 1 // modulus (division remainder)
```

Notify that the division sign gives an incorrect result. This is often because it operates on two integer values and can, therefore, around the result and return an integer. To urge the right value, one among the numbers must be converted into a number.

```
x = 3 / (float) 2; // 1.5
```

## Assignment operators

The second group is that the assignment operators. Most significantly, the assignment operator (=) itself, which assigns a worth to a variable.

## Combined assignment operators

A common use of the assignment and arithmetic operators is to work on a variable then to save lots of the result back to that very same variable. These operations are often shortened with the combined assignment operators.

```
int x = 0;

x += 5; // x = x+5; x -= 5; // x = x-5; x *= 5; // x = x*5; x /= 5; // x = x/5; x %= 5; // x = x%5;
```

## Increment and decrement operators

Another normal operation is to increment or decrement a variable by one. This will be simplified with the increment (++) and decrement (—) operators.

```
x++; // x = x+1; x—; // x = x-1;
```

Both of those operators are often used either before or after a variable.

x++; // post-increment x—; // post-decrement

++x; // pre-increment

—x; // pre-decrement

The result of the variable is the same whichever is employed. The difference is that the post-operator returns the first value before it changes the variable, while the pre-operator changes the variable first then return the worth.

x = 5; y = x++; // y=5, x=6 x = 5; y = ++x; // y=6, x=6

## Comparison operators

The comparison operators connect two values and return either true or false. They're mainly wont to specify conditions, which are expressions that evaluate to either true or false.

bool x = (1 == 3); // false // adequate to

x = (4! = 3); // true // not adequate to x = (3 > 4); // false // greater than x = (3 < 4); // true // but

x = (3 >= 4); // false // greater than or adequate to x = (2 > 1 = 10 (2) // right shift x = ~4; // ~00000100 = 11111011 (-5) // invert

These bitwise operators have shorthand assignment operators, a bit like the arithmetic operators.

int x = 5; x &= 5; // 101 & 100 = 100 (4) // and

x=5; x |= 5; // 101 | 100 = 101 (5) // or

x=5; x ^= 5; // 101 ^ 100 = 001 (1) // xor

**x=5; x > 1 = 10 (2) // right shift**

## operator precedents

In C#, expressions are normally evaluated from left to right. However, when an expression contains multiple operators, the precedence of these operators decides the order during which they're evaluated

Pre operator  Pre operator

1   ++—! ~   7   &

2   * / %   8   ^

3   + -   9   |

4   << >>     10 &&

5   < <= > >= 11 ||

6   == !=     12 = op=

For example, logical and (&&) binds weaker than relational operators, which successively bind weaker than arithmetic operators.

Bool x = 2 + 4 > 1 * 4 && 5 / 5 == 1; // true

To make things clearer, parentheses are often wont to specify which a part of the expression is going to be evaluated first. Parentheses have the very best precedence of all operators.

Bool x = ((2 + 5) > (1 * 4)) && ((5 / 5) == 1); // tru e

# Chapter 5
# String

The string data type is employed to store string constants, which are delimited by a quotation marks.

String a = "Hello";

## String concatenation

The sign is employed to mix two strings. It's referred to as the concatenation operator (+) during this context. It also has an accompanying assignment operator (+=), which appends a string to a different and creates a replacement string.

String b = a + "World"; // Hello World b += "World" ; // Hello World

## Escape characters

A statement are often choppy across multiple lines, but a string constant must get on one line. So as to divide it, the string constant has got to first be break up using the concatenation operator.

String c = "Hello" + "World";

To add new lines into the string itself, the escape character "\n" is employed.

String c = "Hello\nWorld";

This backslash notation is employed to write down special characters, like the backslash itself or a double-quote. Among the special characters is additionally a Unicode character notation for writing any character.

| Character | Meaning | Character | Meaning |
| --- | --- | --- | --- |
| \n | newline | \f | form feed |
| \t | horizontal tab | \a | alert sound |
| \v | vertical tab | \' | single quote |
| \b | backspace | \" | double quote |
| \r | carriage return | \\ | backslash |
| \0 | null character | \uFFFF | Unicode character (4-digit hex number) |

Escape characters may be unheeded by adding associate degree "" symbol before the string. This is often known as a verbatim string and might as an example be accustomed create file ways additional decipherable.

string e = "c:\\Windows\\System32\\cmd.exe";

string f = "c:\Windows\System32\cmd.exe";

**String compare**

The thanks to compare two strings is just by using the adequate to operator. This may not compare the memory addresses, as in another languages like Java.

bool c = (a == b); // true

**String members**

The string class features a lot of useful members. For instance, methods like Replace, Insert and take away. A crucial thing to notice is that there are not any methods for changing a string. Methods that appear to switch a string actually always return a totally new string.

This is because the string class is immutable. The content of a string variable can't be changed, unless the entire string is replaced.

string a = "String" ;

string b = a.Replace( "i" , "o" ); // Strong

b = a.Insert(0, "My " ); // My String b = a.Remove(0, 3);  // ing

b = a.Substring(0, 3);  // Str

**b = a.ToUpper(); // STRING int  i = a.Length;  // 6**

**StringBuilder class**

StringBuilder is a mutable string class. Because of the performance cost related to replacing a string, the StringBuilder class may be a better alternative when a string must be modified repeatedly.

System.Text.StringBuilder sb = new System.Text.StringBuilder("Hello");

The class has several methods which will be wont to manipulate the particular content of a string, such as Append, Remove and Insert.

sb.Append(" World"); // Hello World sb.Remove(0, 6); // World sb.Insert(0, "Bye"); // Bye World

To convert a StringBuilder object back to a daily string, the ToString method is employed.

```csharp
string s = sb.ToString(); // Bye World
```

# Chapter 6

# Arrays

An array may be a arrangement used for storing a set of values that each one have an equivalent data type.

**Array declaration**

To declare an array, a group of square brackets is appended to the info type the array will contain, followed by the array's name. An array is often declared with any data type and every one of its elements will then be of that type.

```
int[] x; // not int x[]
```

**Array allocation**

The array is allocated with the new keyword, followed again by the info type and a group of square brackets containing the length of the array. This is often the fixed number of elements that the array can contain. once the array is made, the weather will automatically be assigned to the default value for that data type.

```
int[] x = new int[3];
```

**Array assignment**

To fill the array elements they will be referenced one at a time then assigned values. An array element is referenced by locating the element's index inside square brackets.

Notice that the index for the primary element starts with zero.

```
x[0] = 1;
```

```
x[1] = 2;
```

```
x[2] = 3;
```

Alternatively, the values are often assigned all directly by employing a curly bracket notation. The New keyword and data type may optionally be overlooked if the array is said at an equivalent time.

```
int[] y = new int[] { 1, 2, 3,4 };
```

```
int[] z = { 1, 2, 3,4 };
```

**Array access**

once the array elements are initialized, they will be accessed by referencing the elements' indexes inside the square brackets.

System.Console.Write(x [0] + x [1] + x [2]); // 8

## Rectangular arrays

There are two sorts of multi-dimensional arrays in C#: rectangular and jagged. A rectangular array has an equivalent length of all sub-arrays and separates the size employing a comma.

string[,] x = new string[2, 2];

As with single-dimensional arrays, they will either be filled in one at a time or all directly during the allocation.

x[0, 0] = "00"; x[0, 1] = "01";

x[1, 0] = "10"; x[1, 1] = "11";

## Jagged arrays

Jagged arrays are arrays of arrays, and may have irregular dimensions. The size is allocated one at a time and therefore the sub-arrays can therefore be allocated to different sizes.

string[][] a = new string[2][];

a[0] = new string[1]; a[0][0] = "00";

a[1] = new string[2]; a[1][0] = "10"; a[1][1] = "11";

It is possible to assign the values during the allocation.

string[][] b = { new string[] { "00" },

new string[] { "10", "11" } };

These are all samples of two-dimensional arrays. If quite two dimensions are needed, more commas are often added for the oblong array, or more square brackets for the jagged array.

# Chapter 7
# Conditionals

Conditional statements are wont to execute different code blocks supported different conditions.

**If statement**

If statement will only perform if the condition inside the parentheses is evaluated to true.

```
int x = new System.Random().Next(3); // gives 0, 1 or 3

if (x < 1) {

System.Console.Write(x + " < 1" );

}
```

To test for other conditions, if statement is often extended by any number of else if-clauses. Each additional condition will only be examined if all past conditions are false.

```
else if (x > 2) {

System.Console.Write(x + " > 2" );

}
```

If statement can have one else clause at the top, which can execute if all previous conditions are false.

```
Else {

System.Console.Write(x + "== 1 ");

}
```

As for the curly brackets, they will be overlooked if only one statement must be executed conditionally.

```
if (x< 1)

System.Console.Write(x + " < 2" );

else if (x > 2)

System.Console.Write(x + " > 1" );

else
```

System.Console.Write(x + "== 1");

## Switch statement

The switch statement checks for equality between either an integer or a string and a series of case labels, then passes execution to the matching case. The statement can contain any number of case clauses and should end with a default label for handling all other cases.

```
int x = new System.Random().Next(3); // gives 0, 1 or 3

switch (x)

{

default :System.Console.Write(x + " is 2" );

break ;

}
```

Note that the statements after each case label aren't surrounded by curly brackets.

Instead, the statements end with the break keyword to interrupt out of the switch. Unlike many other languages, case clauses in C# must end with a jump statement, like a break. This suggests that the break keyword can't be overlooked to permit the execution to fall-through to the subsequent label. The rationale for this is often that unintentional fall-throughs may be a common software error.

## Go to statement

To cause a fall-through to occur, this behavior has got to be explicitly specified using the go to jump statement followed by a case label. This may cause the execution to leap thereto label.

Case 0: goto case 1;

Goto could also be used outside of switches to leap to a label within an equivalent method's scope. Control may then be transported out of a nested scope, but not in a nested scope. However, using goto during this manner is discouraged since it can become difficult to follow the flow of execution.

goto myLabel;

// ... myLabel:

## Ternary operator

In addition to if and switch statements there's the ternary operator (? :). This operator can replace one if/else clause that assigns a worth to a selected variable. The operator takes three expressions. If the primary one is evaluated to true then the second expression is returned, and if it's false, the third one is returned.

```
// Value between 0.0 and 1.0

Double x = new System.Random().NextDouble();

x = (x< 0.5)? 0: 1; // ternary operator (? :)
```

# Chapter 8
# Loops

There square measure four process structures in C#. These square measure used to execute a specific code block multiple times. While with the conditional if statement, the frizzly brackets for the loops square measure usually unnoted if there is only 1 statement inside the code block.

**While loop**

The whereas loop runs through the code block as long as its condition is true, and might continue process for as long as a result of the condition remains true. Note that the condition is simply checked at the beginning of each iteration (loop).

int i = 0;

While (i < 10) // 0-9

**Do-while loop**

The do-while loop works inside a similar manner as a result of the whereas loop, except that it checks the condition when the code block and might thus continually run through the code block a minimum of once. Bear in mind that this loop ends with a punctuation mark.

int j = 0;

Do whereas (j < 10); // 0-9

**For loop**

For loop is used to travel through a code block a specific range of times. It uses 3 parameters. The first parameter initializes a counter and is typically dead once, before the loop. The second parameter holds the condition for the loop and is checked before every iteration. The third parameter contains the increment of the counter and is dead at the highest of each iteration.

for (int k = zero; k < 10; k++)

For loop has many variations. As associate degree example, the first and third parameters square measure usually split into many statements victimization the comma operator.

for (int k = 0, m = 5; k < 10; k++, m—) five (10x)

}

There is additionally the selection of exploit out one or additional of the parameters. as an example , the third parameter might even be moved into the body of the loop.

for (int k = 0; k < 10;)

**For each loop**

For each loop provides a straightforward because of repeat through arrays. At every iteration resultant part inside the array is allotted to the specified variable (the iterator) and thus the loop continues to execute till it's practiced the complete array.

int [] a = { one, 2, 3 };

foreach (int n in a)

Note that the iterator variable is read-only and will thus not be used to amendment components inside the array.

**Break and continue**

There square measure 2 special keywords which can be used within loops – break and continue. The break keyword ends the loop structure, and continue skips the rest of the current iteration and continues at the start of resultant iteration.

Finish for continue; // begin next iteration

# Chapter 9
# Methods

Methods square measure reusable code blocks which can solely execute once known as.

**Defining strategies**

A method square measure usually created within a class by typewriting void followed by the method's name, a bunch of parentheses and a code block. The void keyword means that the maneuver will not come a value. The naming convention for strategies is that a similar as for categories – a descriptive name with every word ab initio capitalized.

All strategies in C# should belong to a class, which they're the only place wherever statements might even be dead. C# does not have world functions that square measure strategies outlined outside of categories.

**Calling strategies**

The method on top of can print out a text message. To invoke (call) it associate degree instance of the MyApp category should initial be created by victimization the new keyword. The dot operator is then used when the instance's name to access its members, which contains the MyPrint technique.

class MyApp

Howdy World

}

Void MyPrint()

">

}

**Method parameters**

The parentheses that follow the maneuver name square measure used to pass arguments to the maneuver. To undertake to to the current the corresponding parameters should initial be arranged enter the maneuver definition inside the type of a comma separated list of variable declarations.

void MyPrint(string s1, string s2)

A method area unit usually outlined to need any variety of arguments, which they will have any knowledge varieties. Simply make certain the tactic is known as with a similar varieties and variety of arguments.

Static void Main ()

Hallo World

}

To be precise, parameters seem in technique definitions, whereas arguments seem in technique calls. However, the two terms area unit typically used interchangeably.

**Params keyword**

To take a variable variety of arguments of a particular kind, associate in Nursing array with the params modifier area unit usually adscititious as a result of the last parameter at intervals the list. Any further parameters of the desired kind that area unit passed to the maneuver can mechanically be keep in this array.

void MyPrint(params string[] s)

**Method overloading**

It is attainable to declare multiple strategies with a similar name as long as a result of the parameters vary in kind or variety. {This is this is usually this can be} often referred to as technique overloading and will as an example be seen at intervals the implementation of the System.Console.Write technique, that has eighteen technique definitions. it is a robust feature that allows how to handle a variety of arguments while not the technologist eager to keep in mind of victimisation completely different strategies.

void MyPrint(string s)

void MyPrint(int i)

**optional parameters**

As of C# 4.0, parameters area unit usually declared as elective by providing a default worth for them at intervals the tactic declaration. once the maneuver is invoked, these elective arguments might even be omitted to use the default values.

class MyApp{

static void Main()

}

**Named arguments**

C# 4.0 conjointly introduced named arguments, which enable Associate in Nursing argument to be passed victimisation the name of its corresponding parameter. This feature enhances elective parameters by sanctioning arguments to be passed out of order, instead of wishing on their position at intervals the parameter list. Therefore, any elective parameters area unit usually such that while not having to specify the value for every elective parameter before it. Each elective and needed parameters area unit usually named, however the named arguments should be placed once the unidentified ones.

static void Main(){

seven

}

**Return statement**

A method will come back a price. The void keyword is then replaced with the information kind that the maneuver can come back, and thus the comeback keyword is adscititious to the maneuver body with Associate in Nursing argument of the desired come back kind.

String Get Print ()

">

Return is also a jump statement that causes the maneuver to exit and come back the value to the place wherever the maneuver was referred to as. As an example, the Get Print technique on top of area unit usually passed as Associate in nursing argument to the Write technique since the maneuver evaluates to a string.

Static void Main ()

Hullo World

}

The comeback statement may also be used in void strategies to exit before the highest block is reached.

Void My Method ()

**Value and reference varieties**

There are a unit 2 varieties of knowledge varieties in C#: worth varieties and reference varieties. Variables helpful varieties directly contain their knowledge, whereas variables of reference varieties hold references to their knowledge. The reference varieties in C# include: category, interface, array and delegate varieties. The value varieties embrace the easy varieties, conjointly as a result of the struct, enum and nullable varieties. Reference kind variables area unit generally created victimisation the new keyword, although that is not forever necessary, as as an example at intervals the case of string objects.

A variable of a reference kind is typically referred to as Associate in Nursing object, although to be precise the issue is that the info that the variable refers to. With reference varieties, multiple variables will reference a similar object, and therefore operations performed through one variable can have an effect on the opposite variables that reference a similar object. In distinction, with worth varieties, every variable can store its own worth and operations on one will not have an effect on another.

**Pass by worth**

When passing parameters helpful kind solely a part copy of the variable is passed, therefore if the copy is changed it's going to not have an effect on the primary variable.

void Set(int i) static void Main()

{

MyApp m = new MyApp();

int x = 0; // worth kind

m.Set(x); // pass worth of x System.Console.Write(x); // zero

}

**Pass by reference**

For reference knowledge varieties C# uses true pass reference. This means that once a reference kind is passed it is not solely attainable to vary its state, however conjointly to exchange the total object and have the modification propagate back to the primary object.

void Set (int[] i) ten }; } static void Main()

{

MyApp m = new MyApp();

int[] y = { zero }; // reference kind

m.Set(y); // pass object system .Console.Write(y[0]); // ten

}

**Ref keyword**

A variable helpful kind area unit usually elapsed reference by victimization the ref keyword, each at intervals the caller and technique declaration. This might cause the variable to be passed in by reference, and therefore dynamic it's going to update the primary worth.

void Set(ref int i)

static void Main()

{

MyApp m = new MyApp();

int x = 0; // worth kind

m.Set(ref x); // pass reference to worth kind System.Console.Write(x); // ten

}

**out keyword**

Sometimes you will need to pass Associate in Nursing unassigned variable by reference and have it assigned at intervals the tactic. However, victimisation Associate in nursing unassigned native variable can provides a compile-time error. For this instance the out keyword area unit usually used. It's a similar perform as referee, except that the compiler can enable use of the unassigned variable, and it will force you to actually set the variable at intervals the tactic.

# Chapter 10

# Class

A class could be a model accustomed produce objects. They're created of members, the most 2 of that square measure fields and strategies. Fields square measure variables that hold the state of the item, whereas strategies outline what the item will do.

class MyRectangle{

come x * y;

}

**object creation**

To use a category's members from outside the shaping class, associate degree object of the category should initial be created? This is often done by victimization the new keyword, which can produce a replacement object within the system's memory.

class MyClass

{

static void Main()

{

// produce associate degree object of

MyRectangle MyRectangle r = new MyRectangle();

}

}

An object is additionally referred to as associate degree instance. The item can contain its own set of fields, which may hold values that square measure totally different to those of alternative instances of the category.

**Accessing object members**

In addition to making the item, the members of {the category|the category} that square measure to be accessible got to be declared as public within the class definition.

class MyRectangle

build members accessible for instances of the category

public int x, y;

public int GetArea() come back x * y; }

}

The dot operator is employed once the object's name to reference its accessible members.

static void Main(){

fifty

}

**Constructor**

The class will have a creator. This is often a special reasonably methodology accustomed instantiate (construct) the item. It continually has identical name because the category and doesn't have a come kind, as a result of it implicitly returns a replacement instance of the category. To be accessible from another category it has to be declared with the general public access modifier.

public MyRectangle()

When a replacement instance of the category is made the creator methodology is named, that within the example higher than sets the fields to the desired initial values.

static void Main()

The creator will have a parameter list, even as the other methodology. As seen below, this could be accustomed create the fields' initial values rely upon the parameters passed once the item is made.

class MyRectangle

breadth, int height)

static void Main(){

}

**This keyword**

Inside the creator, still as in alternative strategies happiness to the item, a special keyword referred to as this could be used. This keyword could be a relevance this instance of the category. Suppose, as an example, that the constructor's parameters have identical names because the corresponding fields. The fields might then still be accessed by victimization the keyword, even if they're overshadowed by the parameters.

class MyRectangle

}

## Constructor overloading

To support totally different parameter lists the creator is overladen. Within the example below, the fields are going to be appointed default values if the category is instantiated with none arguments. With one argument each fields are going to be set to the desired worth, and with 2 arguments every field are going to be appointed a separate worth. {attempting|trying|making associate degree attempt} to make an object with the incorrect variety of arguments, or with incorrect knowledge sorts, can end in a compile-time error, even as with the other methodology.

public MyRectangle()

public MyRectangle(int a)

public MyRectangle(int a, int b)

## Constructor chaining

The keyword also can be accustomed decision one creator from another. This is often called creator chaining and permits for larger code use. Note that the keyword seems as a way decision before the creator body and once a colon.

public MyRectangle() : this(10,5) public MyRectangle(int a) : this(a,a) public MyRectangle(int a, int b)

## Initial field values

If there square measure fields within the category that require to be appointed initial values, like within the case of the primary creator higher than, the fields will merely be initialized at identical time as they're declared. This could create the code a touch cleaner. The initial values are going to be appointed once the item is made before the creator is named.

class MyRectangle

An assignment of this kind is named a field initializer. Such associate degree assignment cannot discuss with another instance field.

## Default creator

It is attainable to make a category even though no constructor's square measure outlined. This is often as a result of the compiler can mechanically add a default parameter less creator to such a category. The default creator can instantiate the item and set every field to its default worth.

class My Rectangle category MyApp

```
{

static void Main()

{

// Calls default creator MyRectangle r = new MyRectangle();

}

}
```

**object initializers**

When making associate degree object, as of C# 3.0, it's attainable to initialize the object's public fields among the representation statement. A code block is then else, containing

A comma-separated list of field assignments. The item initializer block are going to be processed once the creator has been referred to as.

```
class MyRectangle

class MyClass

{

static void Main()

{

// object initializer

MyRectangle r = new MyRectangle() { x = ten, y = 5 };

}

}
```

If there are not any arguments for the creator, the parentheses could also be removed.

```
MyRectangle r = new MyRectangle { x = ten, y = 5 };
```

**Partial category**

A class definition is separate into separate supply files by victimization the partial kind modifier. These partial categories are going to be combined into the ultimate kind by the compiler. All elements of a partial category should have the partial keyword and share identical access level.

```
// File1.cs
```

public partial category MyPartialClass

// File2.cs

public partial category MyPartialClass

Splitting categories across multiple supply files is primarily helpful once a part of a category is generated mechanically. as an example, this feature is employed by Visual Studio's graphical program builder to separate mechanically generated code from manually written code. Partial categories also can create it easier for multiple programmers to figure on identical categories.

## Garbage collector

The .NET Framework encompasses a garbage man that sporadically releases the memory employed by objects once they are not any longer accessible. This frees the engineer from the usually tedious and erring task of manual memory management. Associate degree object are going to be eligible for destruction once there are not any additional references thereto. This happens, as an example, once an area object variable goes out of scope. Associate degree object cannot be expressly deallocated in C#.

## Destructor

In addition to constructors, a category also can have a destructor. The destructor is employed to unharness any unmanaged resources allotted by the item. It's referred to as mechanically before associate degree object is destroyed, and can't be referred to as expressly. The name of the destructor is that the same because the category name, however preceded by a diacritical mark (~). A category could solely have one destructor and it doesn't take any parameters or come any worth.

class MyComponent

// Destructor

~MyComponent()

}

In general, the .NET Framework garbage man mechanically manages the allocation and unharness of memory for objects. However, once a category uses unmanaged resources – like files, network connections, and program elements – a destructor ought to be accustomed unencumber those resources once they are not any longer required.

## Null keyword

The null keyword is employed to represent a null reference that could be a reference that doesn't discuss with any object. It will solely be appointed to variables of reference kind, and to not worth kind variables. The adequate operator (==) is accustomed check whether or not associate degree object is null.

String s = null;

if (s == null) s = new String();

## Nullable sorts

A value kind is created to carry the worth null additionally to its traditional vary of values by appending an issue mark (?) to its underlying kind. This is often referred to as a null able kind and permits the straightforward sorts, still as alternative struct sorts, to point associate degree vague worth. As an example, boll? Could be a null able kind that may hold the values true, false, and null.

bool? b = null;

## Null-coalescing operator

The null coalescing operator returns the left-hand number if it's not null and unless returns the right-hand quantity. This conditional operator provides a straightforward syntax for assignment a nullable kind to a non-nullable kind.

int? i = null;

int j = i ?? zero; // 0

A variable of a nullable kind mustn't be expressly solid to a non-nullable kind. Doing therefore can cause a software error if the variable has null as its worth.

int j = (int)i; // software error

## Default values

The default worth of a reference kind is null. For the straightforward knowledge sorts the default values square measure as follows: numerical sorts become zero, a char has the Unicode character for zero (\0000) and a bool is fake. Default values are going to be appointed mechanically by the compiler for fields. However, expressly specifying the default worth for fields is taken into account sensible programming since it makes the code easier to grasp. For native variables the default values won't be set by the compiler. Instead, the compiler forces the engineer to assign values to any native variables that square measure used, therefore on avoid issues related to victimization unassigned variables.

class MyApp

{

int x; // field is appointed default worth zero

```
int dummy()
{
int x; // native variable should be appointed if used
}
}
```

# Chapter 11

# Inheritance

Inheritance permits {a category category} to amass the members of another class. Within the example below, the category sq. inherits from parallelogram, nominative by the colon. Parallelogram then becomes the bottom category of sq. that successively becomes a derived category of parallelogram. Additionally to its own members, sq. gains all accessible members in parallelogram, aside from any constructors and destructor.

// Base category (parent category) class parallelogram

{

public int x = ten, y = 10;

public int GetArea() come back x * y;

}

// Derived category (child category) class sq. : parallelogram

**object category**

A category in C# could solely inherit from one base class. If no base category is nominative the category can implicitly inherit from System.object. It's thus the foundation category of all alternative categories.

class parallelogram : System.object

C# encompasses a unified kind system therein all knowledge sorts directly or indirectly inherit from object. This doesn't solely apply to categories, however additionally to alternative knowledge sorts, like arrays and easy sorts. as an example, the int keyword is just associate degree alias for the System.Int32 struct kind. Likewise, object is associate degree alias for the System.object category.

System.object o = new object ();

Because every type inherit from object, all of them share a typical set of strategies. one such methodology is ToString that returns a string illustration of this object.

System.Console.Write( o.ToString() ); // System.object

**Downcast and upcast**

Conceptually, a derived category could be a specialization of the bottom category. This suggests that sq. could be a reasonably parallelogram moreover as associate degree object, and might so be used anyplace a parallelogram or object is anticipated. If the associate degree instance of sq. is formed, it will be air duct to parallelogram since the derived category contains everything within the base category.

Square s = new sq. (); parallelogram r = s;

The object is currently viewed as a parallelogram, therefore solely Rectangle's members will be accessed. once the item is downcast into a sq. everything specific to the sq. category can still be preserved. This is often as a result of the parallelogram solely contained the sq., it failed to modification the sq. object in any method.

Square s2 = (Square) r;

The downcast must be created specific since down casting associate degree actual parallelogram into a sq. isn't allowed.

Rectangle r2 = new parallelogram (); sq. s3 = (Square) r2; // error

**Is keyword**

There are a unit 2 operators which will be accustomed avoid exceptions once casting objects. 1st there's the is operator, that returns true if the left facet object will be solid to the proper facet sort while not inflicting associate degree exception.

Rectangle Q = new Square();

if (q is sq.) // condition is true

**As keyword**

The second operator accustomed avoid object casting exceptions is that the as operator.

This operator provides another method of writing an exact solid, with the distinction that if it fails the reference are set to null.

Rectangle r = new parallelogram ();

Square o = r as sq.; // invalid solid, returns null

**Boxing**

The unified sort system of C# permits for a variable of import sort to be implicitly regenerate into a reference kind of the item category. This operation is understood as boxing and once the worth has been traced into the item it's seen as a reference sort.

int myInt = 5;

object myobj = myInt; // boxing

**Unboxing**

The opposite of boxing is unboxing. This converts the boxed price into a variable of its price sort. The unboxing operation should be specific since if the item isn't unboxed into the proper type A software error can occur.

myInt = (int)myobj; // unboxing

# Chapter 12
# Redefining Members

A member in an exceedingly derived category will redefine a member in its base category. This will be in deep trouble every kind of heritable members, however it's most frequently accustomed provide instance strategies new implementations. To convey a technique a replacement implementation, the tactic is redefined within the kid category with an equivalent signature because it has within the base category. The signature includes the name, parameters and come kind of the tactic.

class parallelogram

one, y = 10;

public int GetArea() { come x * y; }

}

class sq. : parallelogram

{

public int GetArea() { come a pair of * x; }

}

## Hiding members

It should be such whether or not methodology|the tactic|the strategy} is meant to cover or override the heritable method. By default, the new methodology can hide it, however the compiler can provides a warning that the behavior ought to be expressly such. to get rid of the warning the new modifier must be used. This specifies that the intention was to cover the heritable methodology and to switch it with a replacement implementation.

class sq. : parallelogram

{

public new int GetArea() { come a pair of * x; }

}

## overriding members

Before a technique will be overridden, the virtual modifier should 1st be other to the tactic within the base category. This modifier permits the tactic to be overridden in an exceedingly derived category.

class parallelogram

one, y = 10;

public virtual int GetArea() { come x * y; }

}

The override modifier will then be accustomed modification the implementation of the heritable methodology.

class sq. : parallelogram

{

public override int GetArea() { come a pair of * x; }

}

## Hiding and preponderating

The distinction between override and new is shown once a sq. is air duct to a parallelogram. If methodology the tactic strategy is redefined with the new modifier then this permits access to the antecedently hidden method outlined in parallelogram. on the opposite hand, if the tactic is

Redefined victimization the override modifier then the air duct can still decision the version outlined in sq... Basically, the new modifier redefines the tactic down the category hierarchy, whereas override redefines the tactic each up and down within the hierarchy.

## Sealed keyword

To stop associate degree overridden methodology from being additional overridden in categories that inherit from the derived category, the tactic will be declared as sealed to negate the virtual modifier.

class MyClass

}

A category may be declared as sealed to stop any class from inheritable it.

Sealed category no inheritable

## Base keyword

There is the way to access a parent's methodology though it's been redefined. This is often done by victimization the bottom keyword to reference the bottom category instance. Whether or not the tactic is hidden or overridden it will still be reached by victimization this keyword.

```
class Triangle : parallelogram

{

public override GetArea() { come base.GetArea()/2; }

}
```

The base keyword may be accustomed decision a base category builder from a derived

Class builder. The keyword is then used as a technique decision before the constructor's body, prefixed by a colon.

```
Class parallelogram

one, y = 10;

public Rectangle(int a, int b)

}

class sq. : parallelogram

{

public Square(int a) : base(a,a)

}
```

When a derived category builder doesn't have an exact decision to the bottom category builder, the compiler can mechanically insert a decision to the parameter less base category builder so as to confirm that the bottom category is correctly made.

```
class sq. : parallelogram

{

public Square(int a) // : base() implicitly other

}
```

Note that if the bottom category contains a builder outlined that's not parameter less, the compiler won't produce a default parameter less builder. Therefore, shaping a builder within the derived category, while not an exact decision to an outlined base category builder, can cause a compile-time error.

```
class Base { public Base(int a) }

class Derived : Base // compile-time error
```

# Chapter 13
# Access Levels

Every category member has associate degree accessibility level that determines wherever the member are visible. There are a unit 5 of them on the market in C#: public, protected, internal, and protected internal and personal. The default access level for members of a category is non-public.

**Private access**

All members in spite of access level area unit accessible within the category during which they're declared, the insertion category. The sole place wherever a non-public member can be accessed.

class MyBase

{

// unrestricted access public int myPublic;

// shaping assembly or derived category protected internal int myProtInt;

// shaping assembly internal int myInternal;

// shaping or derived category protected int myProtected;

// shaping category solely non-public int myPrivate;

void Test()

}

**Protected access**

A protected member may be accessed from among a derived category, however it's inaccessible from different categories.

class Derived : MyBase

}

**Internal access**

An internal member will be accessed anyplace among the native assembly, however not from another assembly. In .NET, associate degree assembly is either a program (.exe) or a library (.dll).

// shaping assembly category AnyClass

}

## Protected internal access

Protected internal access means that either protected or internal. A protected internal member will so be accessed anyplace among this assembly, or in categories outside the assembly that area unit derived from the insertion category.

// different assembly category Derived: MyBase

{

void Test(MyBase m)

}

## Public access

Public access provides unrestricted access from anyplace that the member will be documented.

// different assembly category AnyClass

}

## Top-level access levels

A commanding member could be a sort that's declared outside of the other sorts. In C#, the subsequent sorts will be declared on the top-level: category, interface, strict, enum and delegate. By default, these uncontained members area unit given internal access. To be able to use a commanding member from another assembly the members ought to be marked as public. This is often the sole different access level allowed for commanding members.

Internal category MyInternalClass public category MyPublicClass

## Inner categories

Classes could contain inner categories, which might be set to either one in every of the 5 access levels. The access levels have an equivalent result on inner categories as they are doing on different members.

If the category is inaccessible, it cannot be instantiated or heritable. By default, inner categories area unit non-public, which implies that they'll solely be used among the category wherever they're outlined.

## Class MyBase

{

// Inner categories (nested classes) public class MyPublic

Protected internal category MyProtInt internal category MyInternal protected category MyProtected private class MyPrivate

}

**Access level guideline**

As a suggestion, once selecting associate degree access level it's usually best to use the foremost restrictive level doable. {This is this is often this will be} as a result of the lot of places a member will be accessed the lot of places it can be accessed, incorrectly, that makes the code tougher to rectify. Victimization restrictive access levels will create it easier to switch {the category|the category} while not breaking the code for the other programmer's victimization that class.

# Chapter 14

# Static

The static keyword may be accustomed declare fields ANd ways which will be accessed while not having to form an instance of the category. Static (class) members solely exist in one copy that belongs to the category itself, whereas instance (non-static) member's square measure created as new copies for every new object. This suggests that static ways cannot use instance members since these ways aren't a part of AN instance. on the opposite hand, instance ways will use each static and instance members.

class MyCircle

Three.14 F;

// Instance methodology float GetArea()

// Static/class methodology

static float ComputeArea(float a)

}

**Accessing static members**

To access a static member from outside the category, the category name is employed followed by the dot operator. This operator is that the same because the one accustomed access instance members, however to succeed in them AN object reference is needed. AN object reference can't be accustomed access a static member.

Static void Main ()

**Static ways**

The advantage of static members is that they will be employed by different categories while not having to form AN instance of the category. Fields ought to so be declared static once solely

a single instance of the variable is required. Ways ought to be declared static if they perform a generic operate that's freelance of any instance variables. a decent example of this is often the System.Math class, that provides a mess of mathematical ways.

This category contains solely static members and constants.

Static void Main ()

**Static fields**

Static fields have the advantage that they persist throughout the lifetime of the appliance.

A static variable will so be used, for instance, to record the quantity of times that a technique has been referred to as.

static int count = 0; public static void Dummy()

The default price for a static field can solely be set once before its 1st used.

**Static categories**

A class also can be marked static if it solely contains static members and constant fields. A static category can't be hereditary or instantiated into AN object. Trying to try and do thus can cause a compile-time error.

static category MyCircle

**Static creator**

A static creator will perform any actions required to initialize a category. Typically, these actions involve initializing static fields that can't be initialized as they're declared. This could be necessary if their formatting needs quite one line, or another logic, to be initialized.

class MyClass

part : array) part = i++;

}

}

The static creator, in distinction to the regular instance creator, can solely be run once. This happens mechanically either once AN instance of the category is made, or once a static member of the category is documented. Static constructors can't be referred to as directly and aren't hereditary. Just in case the static fields even have initializers, those initial values are going to be allotted before the static creator is run.

**Extension ways**

A new feature in C# three.0 is extension ways, which give the way to on the face of it add new instance ways to AN existing category outside its definition. AN extension methodology should be outlined as static during a static category and therefore the keyword this is often used on the primary parameter to designate that category to increase.

static category MyExtensions

{

```
// Extension methodology

public static int ToInt(this string s) come back Int32.Parse(s);

}

}
```

The extension methodology is owed for objects of its 1st parameter kind, in this

Case string, as if it had been AN instance methodology of that category. No relation to the static category is required.

```
class MyApp

">

}
```

Because the extension methodology has AN object reference, it will create use of instance members of the category it's extending. However, it cannot use members of that category that square measure inaccessible because of their access level. The good thing about extension ways is that they permit you to "add" ways to a category while not having to change or derive the initial kind.

# Chapter 15

# Properties

Properties in C# give the power to safeguard a field by reading and writing to that through special ways referred to as assessors. They're typically declared as public with an equivalent knowledge kind because the field they're about to shield, followed by the name of the property and a code block that defines the get and set assessors.

class Time

{

private int seconds;

public int sec

{

get come back seconds; } set

}

}

Properties square measure enforced as ways, however used like they're fields.

static void Main()

Note that the discourse price keyword corresponds to the worth allotted to the property.

## Auto-implemented properties

The kind of property wherever they get and set accessors directly correspond to a field is extremely common. as a result of this there's a shorthand means of writing such a property, by going out the accessor code blocks and therefore the personal field. This syntax was introduced in C# three.0 ANd is named an auto-implemented property.

class Time

}

## Property blessings

Since there's no special logic within the property higher than, it's functionally an equivalent as if it had been a public field. However, as a general rule public fields ought to ne'er be employed in world programming as a result of the various blessings that properties bring.

First of all, properties enable a technologist to vary the interior implementation of the property while not breaking any programs that square measure mistreatment it. This is often of specific importance for printed categories, which can be in use by different programmers. Within the Time category for instance, the field's knowledge kind may need to be modified from in to computer memory unit. With properties, this conversion might be handled within the background. With a public field, however, ever-changing the underlying knowledge kind for a broadcast category can possible break any programs that square measure mistreatment the category.

class Time

{

private computer memory unit seconds;

public int sec

set

}

}

A second advantage of properties is that they permit the technologist to validate the information before permitting an amendment. For instance, the second's field may be prevented from being allotted a negative price.

set\

Properties don't have to correspond to AN actual field. They will even as well reckon their own values. The information might even come back from outside the category, like from a information. There's conjointly nothing that stops the technologist from doing different things within the assessors, like keeping AN update counter.

Public into hour

Set

{

seconds = price * 3600; count++;

}

}

private int count = 0;

**Read-only and write-only properties**

Either one among the assessors may be disregarded. While not the set accessory the property becomes read-only, and by going out the get access or instead the property is formed write-only.

// Read-only property personal into sec

{

public get come back seconds; }

}

// Write-only property personal int sec

{

public set

}

**Property access levels**

The accessory's access levels may be restricted. as an example, by creating the set property personal.

private set

The access level of the property itself also can be modified to limit each assessors.

By default, the accessors square measure public and therefore the property itself is personal.

private int sec

# Chapter 16

# Indexers

Indexers enable AN object to be treated as AN array. They're declared within the same means as properties, except that the keyword is employed rather than a reputation and their accessors take parameters. Within the example below, the skilled worker corresponds to AN object array referred to as knowledge that the style of the skilled worker is ready to object.

class MyArray

{

object[] knowledge = new object[10];

public object this[int i]

set

}

}

The get accessor returns the desired part from the article array, and therefore the set accessor inserts the worth into the desired part. With the skilled worker in situ AN instance of this category may be created ANd used as an array, each to induce and set the weather.

static void Main()

object o = a[5]; //{hello|hullo|hi|howdy|how-do-you-do|greeting|salutation">hi World}

**Indexer parameters**

The parameter list of A skilled worker is comparable thereto of a technique, except that it should have a minimum of one parameter which the official or out modifiers aren't allowed. For instance, if there's a two-dimensional array, the column and row indexes may be passed as separate parameters.

class MyArray

{

object[,] knowledge = new object[10,10];

public object this[int i, int j]

{

get come back data[i,j]; } set

}

}

The index parameter doesn't have to be of a whole number kind. AN object will even as somewhat be passed because the index parameter. The get accessor will then be accustomed come back the index position wherever the past object is found.

class MyArray

{

object[] knowledge = new object[10];

public int this[object o]

{

get come back System.Array.Indexof(data, o); }

}

}

**Indexer overloading**

Both of those functionalities may be provided by overloading the skilled worker. The kind and variety of arguments can then verify that skilled worker gets referred to as.

class MyArray

{

object[] knowledge = new object[10];

public int this[object o]

{

get come back System.Array.Indexof(data, o); }

}

public object this[int i]

{

get come back data[i]; } set

}

}

Keep in mind that during a real program a spread check ought to be enclosed within the accessors, thus on avoid exceptions caused by making an attempt to travel on the far side the length of the array.

public object this[int i]

zero && i < knowledge.Length) ? data[i] : null;

}

Set zero && i < knowledge.Length) data[i] = value;

}

}

# Chapter 17

# Interface

An interface is employed to specify members that derivation categories should implement. They're outlined with the interface keyword followed by a reputation and a code block. Their naming convention is to start out with a capital "I" and so to possess every word ab initio capitalized.

interface IMyInterface

Interface signatures

The interface code block will solely contain signatures, and solely those of ways, properties, indexers and events. The interface members cannot have any implementations. Instead, their bodies square measure replaced by semicolons. They conjointly cannot have any access modifiers since interface member's square measure continually public.

interface IMyInterface

{

// Interface methodology int GetArea();

// Interface property int space

// Interface skilled worker

int this[int index]

// Interface event

Event System.EventHandler MyEvent;

}

Static object Largest (IComparable a, IComparable b)

**Class interface**

A second thanks to use associate interface is to supply associate actual interface for a category, through that the category may be used. Such associate interface defines the practicality that programmer's victimization the category can want.

interface IMyClass

class MyClass : IMyClass

public void Hidden()

}

The programmers will then read instances of the category through this interface, by insertion the objects in variables of the interface sort.

IMyInterface m = new MyClass();

This abstraction provides 2 edges. First, it makes it easier for alternative programmers to use the category since they currently solely have access to the members that ar relevant to them. Second, it makes the category additional versatile since its implementation will modification while not being noticeable by alternative programmer's victimization the category, as long because the interface is followed.

# Chapter 18
# Abstract

An abstract category provides a partial implementation that alternative categories will devolve on. once a category is asserted as abstract it implies that the category will contain incomplete members that has to be enforced in derived categories, additionally to traditional category members.

**Abstract members**

Any member that needs a body may be declared abstract – like strategies, properties and indexers. These members ar then left unimplemented and solely specify their signatures, whereas their bodies ar replaced by semicolons.

abstract category form

technique

public abstract int GetArea();

// Abstract property

public abstract int space

// Abstract trained worker

public abstract int this[int index]

// Abstract event

public delegate void MyDelegate();

public abstract event MyDelegate MyEvent;

// Abstract category

public abstract category InnerShape ;

}

Abstract example

As associate example, the category below has associate abstract methodology named GetArea.

abstract category form

one hundred, y = 100; public abstract int GetArea();

}

If {a category|a category} derives from this abstract class it's then forced to override the abstract member. This is often completely different from the virtual modifier, which specifies that the member is also overridden.

Class parallelogram: form

come back x * y; }

}

The derivation category may be declared abstract likewise, within which case it doesn't have to implement any of the abstract members.

Abstract category parallelogram: form an abstract category also can inherit from a non-abstract category.

class NonAbstract

Abstract category Abstract: Non Abstract if the bottom category has virtual members, these may be overridden as abstract to force any derivation categories to supply new implementations for them.

class MyClass

{

void virtual Dummy()

}

abstract category Abstract : MyClass

{

void abstract override Dummy()

}

An abstract category may be used as associate interface to carry objects made of derived categories.

Shape s = new Rectangle();

It is impracticable to instantiate associate abstract category. Even so, associate abstract category might have constructors which will be known as from derived categories by victimization the bottom keyword.

Shape s = new form(); // compile-time error

## Abstract categories and interfaces

Abstract categories are like interfaces in many ways. They'll each outline member signatures that derivation categories should implement, and neither one in every of them may be instantiated. The key variations are 1st that the abstract category will contain non-abstract members, whereas the interface cannot. And second, that {a category} will implement any range of interfaces however solely inherit from one class, abstract or not.

// Defines default practicality and definitions abstract category form

one hundred, y = 100; public abstract int GetArea();

}

class parallelogram : form // category may be a form

// Defines associate interface or a particular practicality interface IComparable

class MyClass : IComparable // category may be compared

An abstract category will, even as a non-abstract category, extend one base category and implement any range of interfaces. Associate interface, however, cannot inherit from a category. Though it will inherit from another interface that effectively combines the 2 interfaces into one.

# Chapter 19

# Namespaces

Namespaces offer the simplest way to cluster connected ranking members into a hierarchy. They're additionally accustomed avoid naming conflicts. A ranking member, like a category, that's not enclosed during a namespace is claimed to belong to the default namespace. It may be touched to a different namespace by being fenced in during a namespace block. The naming convention for namespaces is that the same as for categories, with every word at first capitalized.

```
namespace MyNamespace

{

class MyClass

}
```

**Nested namespaces**

Namespaces may be nested any range of levels deep to any outline the namespace hierarchy.

```
namespace MyNamespace

{

namespace NestedNamespace

{

class MyClass

}

}
```

A faster thanks to write this is often to merely separate the namespaces with a dot.

```
namespace MyNamespace.NestedNamespace

{

class MyClass

}
```

Note that declaring a similar namespace once more in another category within the project has a similar impact as if each namespaces were enclosed within the same block, although the category is found in another code file.

**Namespace access**

To access a category from another namespace its absolutely qualified name must be specified.

namespace MyNamespace.NestedNamespace

{

public category MyClass

}

namespace otherNamespace

}

}

**Using directive**

The absolutely qualified name may be shortened by together with the namespace with a victimization directive. The members of that namespace will then be accessed anyplace within the code file while not having to prepend the namespace to each reference. It's obligatory to position victimization directives before all alternative members within the code file.

Using MyNamespace.NestedNamespace;

Having direct access to those members implies that if there's a conflicting member signature within the current namespace the member within the enclosed namespace are hidden. As an example, if there's a MyClass within the otherNamespace likewise, that category are employed by default. To use the category within the enclosed namespace, the absolutely qualified name would once more got to be specified.

Using MyNamespace.NestedNamespace; namespace MyNamespace.NestedNamespace

{

Public category MyClass

namespace otherNamespace

{

public category MyClass

}

}

To change this reference, the victimization directive will instead be modified to assign the namespace to associate alias.

using MyAlias = MyNamespace.NestedNamespace;

*// ...*

int x = MyAlias.MyClass.x;

An even shorter manner would be to outline the absolutely qualified category name as a brand new sort for the code file, by victimization a similar alias notation.

Using MyType = MyNamespace.NestedNamespace.MyClass;

*// ...*

int x = MyType.x

# Chapter 20

# Enum

An enumeration may be a special quite price sort consisting of an inventory of named constants.

To create one, the enum keyword is employed followed by a reputation and a code block, containing a comma-separated list of constant parts.

enum State ;

This enumeration sort may be accustomed produce variables which will hold these constants.

To assign a worth to the enum variable, the weather ar accessed from the enum as if they were static members of a category.

State s = State.Run;

Enum example

The switch statement provides an honest example of once associate enumeration may be helpful. Compared to victimization standard constants, associate enumeration has the advantage of permitting the computer user to obviously specify what constant values ar allowed. This provides compile-time sort safety, and IntelliSense additionally makes the values easier to recollect.

switch (s)

**Enum constant values**

There is sometimes no have to be compelled to recognize the particular constant values that the constants represent, however generally it should be necessary. By default, the primary part has the worth zero, and every sequential part has one price higher.

enum State

three

};

These default values may be overridden by assignment values to the constants. The values may be computed and don't have to be distinctive.

enum State five

};

## Enum constant sort

The underlying variety of the constant parts is implicitly specified as int, however this will be modified by employing a colon once the enumeration's name followed by the specified number sort.

enum MyEnum : computer memory unit ;

## Enum access levels and scope

The access levels for enumerations are a similar as for categories. They're internal by default, however also can be declared as public. Though enumerations are sometimes outlined at the ranking, they will be contained inside a category. During a category they need personal access by default, and may be set to either one in every of the access levels.

## Enum strategies

An enumeration constant may be forged to associate int and therefore the ToString methodology may be accustomed acquire its name. Most alternative enumeration strategies may be found within the System.Enum class.

static void Main()

{

State s = State.Run;

int i = (int)s; // zero string t = s.ToString(); // Run

# Chapter 21
# Exception Handling

Exception handling permits programmers to modify sudden things that will occur in programs. As AN example, take into account gap a file exploitation the StreamReader category within the System.Io namespace. To envision what types of exceptions this category could throw, you'll hover the pointer over the category name in Visual Studio. For example, the System.Io exceptions FileNotFoundException and DirectoryNotFoundException. If anyone of these exceptions happens, the program can terminate with a slip-up message.

using System; exploitation System.Io;

class ErrorHandling

software error

StreamReader sr = new StreamReader("missing.txt");

}

}

**Try-catch statement**

To avoid blooming the program the exceptions should be caught employing a try-catch statement. This statement consists of a strive block containing the code that will cause the exception, and one or additional catch clauses. If the strive block with success executes, the program can then continue running once the try-catch statement. However, if AN exception happens the execution can then be passed to the primary catch block able to handle that exception kind.

try

">

catch

">

**Catch block**

Since the catch block higher than isn't set to handle any specific exception it'll catch all of them. This is often adore catching the System.Exception category, as a result of all exceptions derive from this category.

catch (Exception)

To catch a additional specific exception the catch block has to be placed before additional general exceptions.

catch (FileNotFoundException) catch (Exception)

The catch block will optionally outline AN exception object which will be accustomed get additional data regarding the exception, like an outline of the error.

catch (Exception e)

">

**Finally block**

As the last clause within the try-catch statement, a finally block may be further. This block is employed to wash up sure resources allotted within strive block. Typically, restricted system resources and graphical elements ought to be free during this means once they're now not required. The code within the finally block can invariably execute, whether or not or not there's AN exception. This may be the case albeit strive block ends with a jump statement, like come back.

In the example used antecedently, the file opened within strive block ought to be closed if it absolutely was with success opened. This is often done properly within the next code section. To be able to access the StreamReader object from the finally clause it should be declared outside of

Strive block. Confine mind that if you forget shut to the stream the rubbish handler can eventually close it for you, however it's an honest observe to try to it yourself.

StreamReader sr = null; strive

">

Catch (FileNotFoundException) finally

The statement higher than is thought as a try-catch-finally statement. The catch block may be unnoticed to make a try-finally statement. This statement won't catch any exceptions. Instead, it'll make sure the correct disposal of any resources allotted within strive block.

This can be helpful if the allotted resource doesn't throw any exceptions. For example, such a category would be icon, within the System.Drawing namespace.

using System.Drawing;

// ...

Bitmap b = null; strive

", Height: " + b.Height);

">

Finally Note that once employing a Console Project a regard to the System. Drawing assembly has to be manually further for those members to be accessible. To try to thus right click the References folder within the answer person window and choose Add References. Then from the .NET tab choose the System. Drawing assembly and click on okay to add its regard to your project.

## Using statement

The exploitation statement provides an easier syntax for writing the try-finally statement. This statement starts with the exploitation keyword followed by the resource to be no heritable,

Specified in parentheses. It then includes a code block during which the obtained resource may be used. once the code block has finished execution, the Dispose methodology of the item

Is mechanically referred to as to wash it up. This methodology comes from the System. Disposable

Interface, that the resource should implement this interface. The code below performs identical operate because the one within the previous example, however with fewer lines of code.

Using System. Drawing;

// ...

using (Bitmap b = new Bitmap(100, 100))

", Height: " + b.Height);

">

## Throwing exceptions

When a scenario happens that a technique will not pass though it can generate AN exception to signal the caller that the strategy has unsuccessful. This is often done exploitation the throw keyword followed by a brand new instance of a category explanation from System. Exception.

static void MakeError()

">

The exception can then propagate up the caller stack till it's caught. If a caller catches the exception however isn't able to pass through it, the exception may be re-thrown exploitation solely the throw keyword.

static void Main()

catch

}

If there are not any additional try-catch statements the program can stop execution and show the error message.

# Chapter 22

# operator overloading

operator overloading permits operators to be redefined and used wherever one or each of the operands square measure of an exact category. once done properly, this could alter the code and build user-defined sorts as straightforward to use because the straightforward sorts.

**operator overloading example**

In this example, there's a category referred to as MyNum with A whole number field and a creator for setting that field. There's additionally a static Add methodology that adds 2 MyNum objects along and returns the result as a brand new MyNum object.

class MyNum

public static MyNum Add(MyNum a, MyNum b) { come back new MyNum(a.val + b.val);

}

}

Two MyNum instances may be further along exploitation the Add methodology.

**Binary operator overloading**

What operator overloading will is to alter this syntax and thereby give a additional intuitive interface for the category. To convert the Add methodology to AN overload methodology for the addition sign, replace the name of the strategy with the operator keyword followed by the operator that's to be full. The whitespace between the keyword and therefore the operator will optionally be unnoticed. Note that for AN operator overloading methodology to figure, it should be outlined as each public and static.

class MyNum

public static MyNum operator +(MyNum a, MyNum b)

}

Since the category currently overloads the addition sign this operator may be accustomed perform the desired calculation.

MyNum a = new MyNum(10), b = new MyNum(5); MyNum c = a + b;

**Unary operator overloading**

Addition could be a binary operator, as a result of it takes 2 operands. To overload a single operator, like increment (++), one methodology parameter is employed instead.

public static MyNum operator ++(MyNum a)

Note that this may overload each the termination and prefix versions of the increment operator.

MyNum a = new MyNum(10); a++;

++a;

**Return sorts and parameters**

When overloading a single operator the comeback kind and parameter kind should be of the intromission kind. on the opposite hand, once overloading most binary operators the comeback kind may be something, apart from void, and just one of the parameters should be of the intromission kind. This implies that it's doable to any overload a binary operator with different methodology parameters, for example to permit a MyNum and an int to be further along.

public static MyNum operator +(MyNum a, int b)

C# permits overloading of virtually all operators, as may be seen within the table below. The combined assignment operators can't be expressly full. Instead, they square implicitly full once their corresponding arithmetic or bitwise operators are full.

Binary operators Unary operators not overloadable

+ - * / nothing (+= -= *= /= %=)

& | ^ << >> (&= |= ^= <<= >>=)

== != > < >= <=

+ - ! ~ ++—true false && || =. ( ): new as is typeof

Checked unrestrained

The comparison operators, moreover as true and false, should be full in pairs. As an example, overloading the equal operator means the not equal operator additionally has got to be full.

**True and false operator overloading**

Notice within the previous table that true and false square measure thought of to be operators.

By overloading them, objects of the category may be employed in conditional statements wherever the item has to be evaluated as a mathematician kind. once overloading them the comeback sorts should be bool.

class MyNum

public static bool operator true(MyNum a) { come back (a.val != 0);

}

public static bool operator false(MyNum a) { come back (a.val == 0);

}

}

class MyClass

">

}

# Chapter 23

# Custom Conversions

This chapter covers a way to outline custom kind conversions for AN object. As may be seen within the example below, there's a category referred to as MyNum with one int field and

A creator. With a custom kind conversion, it's doable to permit AN int to be implicitly converted to AN object of this category.

class MyNum

}

**Implicit conversion ways**

For this to figure AN implicit conversion methodology has to be further to the category. This method's signature appearance just like that used for single operator overloading. It should be declared as public static and includes the operator keyword. However, rather than AN operator image the comeback kind is such, that is that the target kind for the conversion. The only parameter can hold the worth that's to be regenerate. The implicit keyword is additionally enclosed, that specifies that the strategy is employed to perform implicit conversions.

Public static implicit operator MyNum(int a)

With this methodology in situ AN int may be implicitly regenerate to a MyNum object.

MyNum a = 5;

Another conversion methodology may be further that handles conversions within the wrong way, from a MyNum object to AN int.

public static implicit operator int(MyNum a)

**Explicit conversion ways**

To prevent probably unplanned object kind conversions by the compiler, the conversion methodology may be declared as specific rather than implicit.

public static specific operator int(MyNum a)

The explicit keyword means the engineer has got to specify an exact forged so as to invoke the sort conversion methodology. Particularly, specific conversion ways ought to be used if the results of the conversion ends up in loss of data, or if the conversion methodology could throw exceptions.

```
MyNum a = 5; int i = (int)a;
```

# Chapter 24
# Delegates

A delegate could be a kind accustomed reference a way. This enables ways to be allotted to variables and passed as arguments. The delegate's declaration specifies the strategy signature to that objects of the delegate kind will refer. Delegates ar by convention named with every word at first capitalized followed by "Delegate" at the top of the name.

delegate void MyDelegate(string s);

A method that matches the delegate's signature are often allotted to a delegate object of this kind.

class MyClass

static void Main()

}

This delegate object can behave as if it absolutely was the strategy itself, regardless of whether or not it refers to a static or associate degree instance technique. A way turn the item are forwarded by the delegate to the strategy, and any come back price are passed back through the delegate.

MyDelegate d = Print; d ("Hello");

The syntax used on top of too instantiate the delegate is really a simplified notation that was introduced in C# a pair of.0. The backwards compatible thanks to instantiate a delegate is to use the regular reference kind format syntax.

MyDelegate d = new MyDelegate(Print);

**Anonymous ways**

C# 2.0 conjointly introduced anonymous ways, which might be allotted to delegate objects. Associate degree anonymous technique is such by victimization the delegate keyword followed by a way parameter list and body. This will change the delegate's internal representation since a separate technique ought not to be outlined so as to instantiate the delegate.

MyDelegate f = delegate (string t);

**Lambda expressions**

C# 3.0 went one step any and introduced lambda expressions. They succeed an equivalent goal as anonymous ways, however with a additional compendious syntax. A lambda expression is written as a parameter list followed by the lambda operator (=>) associate degreed an expression.

delegate int MyDelegate(int i); static void Main()

{

// Anonymous technique

del a = delegate(int x) { come back x * x; };

// Lambda expression

del b = (int x) => x * x;

a(5); // twenty five

b(5); // twenty five

}

The lambda should match the signature of the delegate. Typically, the compiler will confirm the info style of the parameters from the context, in order that they ought not to be such. The parentheses may be unnoticed if the lambda has only 1 input parameter.

del c = x => x * x;

If no input parameters ar required associate degree empty set of parentheses should be such.

delegate void MyEmptyDelegate();

// ...

MyEmptyDelegate d = () => System.Console.Write("Hello");

A lambda expression that solely executes one statement is termed associate degree expression lambda. The expression of a lambda also can be self-enclosed in nappy brackets to permit it to contain multiple statements. This kind is termed an announcement lambda.

MyDelegate e = (int x) =>;

**Multicast delegates**

It is attainable for a delegate object to talk over with quite one technique. Such associate degree object is thought as a multicast delegate and therefore the ways it refers to are contained during a thus referred to as invocation list. To feature another technique to the delegate's invocation list, either the addition operator or the addition assignment operator are often used.

static void Hi() static void Bye()

// ...

d += Bye;

Similarly, to get rid of a way from the invocation list, the subtraction or subtraction assignment operators are used.

d -= Hi;

When business a multicast delegate object, all ways in its invocation list are invoked with an equivalent arguments within the order that they were intercalary to the list.

d(); // HiBye

If the delegate returns a price, solely the worth of the last invoked technique are came back. Likewise, if the delegate has associate degree out parameter, its final price are the worth allotted by the last technique.

**Delegate signature**

As mentioned before, a way are often allotted to a delegate object if it matches the delegate's signature. However, a way ought not to match the signature specifically. A delegate object also can talk over with a way that includes a additional derived come back kind than that outlined within the delegate, or that has parameter varieties that ar ancestors of the corresponding delegate's parameter varieties.

class Base

class Derived : Base

delegate Base MyDelegate(Derived d); category MyClass

{

static Derived Dummy(Base o) { come back new Derived(); }

static void Main()

}

**Delegates as parameters**

An important property of delegates is that they will be passed as technique parameters. To demonstrate the good thing about this, 2 straightforward categories are outlined. The primary one could be a knowledge storage category referred to as Person DB that has associate degree array containing a few of names. It conjointly includes a technique that takes a delegate object as its argument, and calls that delegate for every name within the array.

delegate void ProcessPersonDelegate(string name); category PersonDB

;

public void Process(ProcessPersonDelegate f)

}

The second category is shopper, which can use the storage category. It's a Main technique that makes associate degree instance of PersonDB, and it calls that object's method technique with a way that's outlined within the shopper category.

class shopper

static void PrintName(string name)

}

The good thing about this approach is that it permits the implementation of the info storage to be separated from the implementation of the info process. The storage category solely handles the storage and has no data of the process that's done on the info.

This allows the storage category to be written during a additional general means than if this category had to implement all of the potential process operations that a shopper might want to perform on the info. With this resolution, the shopper will merely plug its own process code into the prevailing storage category.

# Chapter 25

# Events

Events alter associate degree object to apprise different objects once one thing of interest happens. The item that raises the event is referred the publisher and therefore the objects that handle the event are called subscribers.

## Publisher

To demonstrate the utilization of events the publisher are created initial. This may be a category that inherits from Array List, however this version can raise an occurrence whenever associate degree item is intercalary to the list. Before the event are often created a delegate is required that may hold the subscribers. This might be any reasonably delegate, however the quality style pattern is to use a void delegate that accepts 2 parameters. The primary parameter specifies the supply object of the event, and therefore the second parameter could be a kind that either is or inherits from the System.EventArgs category. This parameter sometimes contains the main points of the event, however during this example there ought not to pass any event knowledge then the bottom Eventers category are used because the parameter's kind.

Public delegate void EventHandlerDelegate(object sender,

System.EventArgs e);

class Publisher : System.Collections.ArrayList

## Event keyword

With the delegate outlined, the event are often created within the Publisher category victimization the event keyword followed by the delegate and therefore the name of the event. The event keyword creates a special reasonably delegate that may solely be invoked from at intervals the category wherever it's declared. Its access level is public so different categories are allowed to take this event. The delegate that follows the event keyword is termed the event delegate. The name of the event is usually a verb. During this case the event are raised when the item has been intercalary therefore the past-tense of the verb "Add" is employed, that is "Added". If a pre-event was created instead, that is raised before the particular event, then the –ing style of the verb would be used, during this case "Adding".

public event EventHandlerDelegate Added;

Alternatively, in situ of this practice event delegate the predefined System.EventHandler delegate might are used. This delegate is a dead ringer for the one outlined antecedently, and is employed within the .NET category libraries for making events that don't have any event knowledge.

**Event caller**

To invoke the event an occurrence caller are often created. The naming convention for this technique is to precede the event's name with the word "on", that during this case becomes "on Added". The strategy has the protected access level to forestall it from being referred to as from associate degree unrelated category, and it's marked as virtual to permit etymologizing categories to override it. It takes the event arguments as its one parameter that during this case is of the EventArgs kind. The strategy can solely raise the event if it's not null, which means only if the event has any registered subscribers. To boost the event the instance reference is passed because the sender, and therefore the EventArgs object is that the object that was passed to the strategy.

Protected virtual void onAdded(System.EventArgs e)

**Raising events**

Now that the category has an occurrence and a way for business it, the ultimate step is to override the ArrayList's Add technique to create it raise the event. During this overridden version of {the technique|the tactic|the strategy} the bottom class's Add method is initial referred to as, and therefore the result's keep. The event is then raised with the onAdded technique, by passing to that the Empty field within the System.EventArgs category that represents an occurrence with no knowledge. Finally, the results came back to the caller.

public override int Add(object value)

{

int i = base.Add(value); onAdded(System.EventArgs.Empty); come back i;

}

The complete publisher category currently has the subsequent look.

class Publisher : System.Collections.ArrayList

{

public delegate void EventHandlerDelegate(object sender,

System.EventArgs e); public event EventHandlerDelegate Added;

protected virtual void onAdded(System.EventArgs e)

public override int Add(object value)

{

int i = base.Add(value); onAdded(System.EventArgs.Empty); come back i;

}

}

## Subscriber

To make use of the publisher category another category are created that may take the event.

class Subscriber

Event handler

This category contains an occurrence handler that could be a technique that has an equivalent signature because the event delegate and is employed to handle an occurrence. The name of the handler is usually the same because the name of the event followed by the "EventHandler" suffix.

class Subscriber

">

}

## Subscribing to events

The publisher and subscriber categories ar currently complete. To demonstrate their use, a Main technique is intercalary wherever objects of the Publisher and Subscriber categories are created.

In order to register the handler within the Subscriber object to the event within the Publisher object, the event handler is intercalary to the event as if it absolutely was a delegate. Not like a delegate, however, the event might not be referred to as directly from outside its containing category. Instead, the event will solely be raised by the Publisher category, that during this case happens once associate degree item is intercalary thereto object.

# Conclusion

You've started the long and often arduous journey of programming in this book. And the best thing about it? There's no finite endpoint. There's never going to be a point in programming where you say enough is enough, or where you reach some kind of "peak" in your knowledge. Well, technically speaking, maybe, but only if you quit trying will you have hit a peak.

Programming is one of the most liberating tasks known to man because it's the ultimate art form. It's the most interactive art form too. When you program, what you're doing is literally talking to the computer, and thereby making the computer talk to the user. Every single program you make is an extension of the effort that you put into it and the time and the code that you've dedicated to it.

Programming, too, is not easy. In fact, it's rather difficult. And there are topics that are sadly too esoteric to cover in this book hope what I've given you is a very solid foundational understanding of C# so that you can better service yourself to learn about these things.

My goal here wasn't explicitly to teach you C# or any of that: my goal was to teach you the computer. The way it thinks, and the way programs are written. Anybody can learn C# keywords. But to learn to program, and to write solid effective code regardless of which programming language that you're using, that's another skill entirely.